GREETINGS FROM BATH

A Collection of Postcards of Bath
c.1900—1940
Compiled & Edited by Felicity Bowers
Introduction by Karl Jaeger

KINGSMEAD PRESS

Introduction

The picture postcard as we know it today appears to go back to 1867 and was introduced in Germany at the time of the North German Postal Confederation. It had many antecedents however, including illustrated engraved stationery of the early 19th Century.

In 1840 when Great Britain issued the first postage stamp, she also issued the so-called "Mulready" envelope with its illustrated border surrounding the space for the address. Almost at once printers began making caricatures of the Mulready design, replacing the British Lion with a mule. Other illustrated envelopes followed advocating various causes such as Ocean Penny Postages and temperance. The American Civil War saw the widespread use of patriotic envelopes in hundreds of different designs, many in multiple colours.

Thus the stage was set for the picture postcard. The advent of photographic processes and the increase in touristic travel completed the ingredients for the sudden "craze" which picture postcards quickly became.

The first International Postal Convention deliberated many hours before deciding to encourage the International use of postcards by setting their postal rate at one half that of a letter. This act furthered the use of postcards throughout the world. In 1902 Britain made it legal for the message and the address to be on the same side of the card, thus freeing one side to be occupied exclusively by the pictures.

Today as we look at these old "views" we cannot help but make comparisons with the scene (or what is left of it) today. Clothing styles, hair styles, modes of transportation all stand out. But careful study also reveals many changes in Bath's pre-postcard buildings.

We hope that this "souvenir of Bath" may add interest to your visit and contribute to your memories and fantasies as well. We appreciate the help of all those Bath citizens who helped with the assembly of these cards and especially Miss Dorothy Mellish for her early encouragement and James Matthews for his advice on the text. Felicity Bowers carried my initial efforts forward to completion and did the invaluable research for and preparation of the captions.

Karl Jaeger

Notes to the Second Edition

No city stands still, least of all an active one like Bath. As a consequence changes affecting some of the captions have occurred since the first edition of this book and the main ones are embodied in the notes given below:

5 The National Trust gift shop was opened in 1976.

10/11 The fountain in the second illustration was removed in the course of recent archaeological excavations.

13 The local evening paper paid for the restoration of the fountain in the 1970s. Although it is no longer possible for the citizens of Bath to take freely of the waters, this situation may be remedied in the future.

14 The treatment centre was closed in 1976 and its fate has since been the centre of much controversy.

19/20 H. & R. Marsh's shop no longer exists.

22 The former station is now part of a supermarket development which has retained its best features.

24 The theatre has recently been completely restored and refurbished, and a new fly tower built, at a cost of around one million pounds.

25 The Queen Square railings, removed during World War II, have now been replaced, lessening the traffic of feet across the grass.

28 The references to left and right should be reversed.

39 The fountain has now been replaced by one of modern design.

40 The former Pulteney Hotel premises are now luxury flats.

44 There have been further changes to the once exotic site of Vilven's shop.

49 Sampson's chemists shop has now changed its function.

50 The hardware shop had become a furniture showroom by 1976.

54 The post office closed in 1984 and other changes have now affected the chemist's shop and the greengrocer's.

55/56 Times and extent of access to the tower may vary and intending visitors are advised to check in advance.

75 Extensive excavations in the cellars recently have produced many interesting finds which have been incorporated in a small museum open to the public.

77 Most of the trees have now gone and the Sports & Leisure Centre has been built on the left.

87 The location may have been the old city gaol, with the Poor School attached.

89 The canal restoration work has continued.

Kingsmead Press
Annesley House, 21 Southside,
Weston-super-Mare, Avon BS23 2QU

ISBN 1 85026 004 4

Revised edition 1986

Printed at The Bath Press, Avon

1/2 The present Bath Abbey was built on the site of the nave of the Norman cathedral, which was in disrepair by the end of the fifteenth century. Rebuilding was instigated by Bishop Oliver King, in 1499. He engaged the Masons Robert and William Verture. (Oliver King's dream, which inspired the rebuilding of the Abbey is illustrated on the west front by angels climbing ladders, as seen overleaf).

After the dissolution of the monasteries the Abbey was again in a bad state of repair. Shocked by its condition whilst on a visit to Bath in 1574, Elizabeth I ordered a national fund to pay for restoration.

In the 1830's several houses, which were boxing the Abbey in, were removed. A parapet, flying buttresses and pinnacles were added.

3/4 In August 1904 one of these pinnacles was struck by lightning. On examination of the badly damaged pinnacle it was found that the others were unsafe as well. It was decided to replace the pinnacles with new ones of a lighter design which, it was claimed, returned more to the original character of the overall design of the Abbey. There was quite a controversy about whether there should, in fact, be any pinnacles at all, but the conclusion was that the designer had originally intended there to be pinnacles, as the tops of the towers did not taper to counteract the optical illusion of their spreading out when seen from the ground.

In 1906 the pinnacles were completed to a design by J. G. Jackson R.A. and built by Hayward & Wooster; three financed by public subscription and one a private gift.

The two cards on the opposite page show the Abbey as it was pre-1904 and this page shows the new design and building work in progress.

5 Marshall Wade's house in the Abbey Churchyard.
Marshall Wade was the commander of the troops who took charge of Bath in 1715 to put an end to the proposed Jacobite rebellion being planned there. This was his first contact with the city but he took up residence there soon after and became MP for Bath in 1722. It is said he gave his illegitimate daughter's hand in marriage to Ralph Allen in recognition of his help in the anti-Jacobite activities. Wade died a bachelor so his fortune went to swell Mr Allen's already considerable one.

Tradition has it that Lord Burlington designed this house in Abbey Churchyard, but the architecture suggests that it is more likely to have been Greenway, who also designed St John's Court (where Beau Nash resided for a time).

The Bible Society's shop remained here until the 1930's. Last year the National Trust opened their gift shop here.

6 Bath chairman in the Abbey Churchyard.
A familiar part of Victorian and Edwardian life in Bath, there were often up to fifty chairmen outside the Pump Room. In Victorian times there were more than 160 licensed chairs in the city. Bath chairs were designed for transporting invalids to and from their treatments. They were virtually airtight with the glass front closed so that they would keep out chills. Chairs took not only invalids but also all kinds of people everywhere. The last chairman, Ernest Ball, retired just after the second world war. The Corporation would not subsidise any more chairs after this so a characteristic feature of Bath life disappeared.

7 Produced by a London printer, this card would probably have been on sale at a number of other spas, overprinted with a different name. Although full-colour printing had been generally used since the end of the last century this card, sent in 1913, was, like many others, hand-coloured. Even at this late date it was more convenient and economical, when only a few tints were needed, to employ young girls to fill them in.

8 Afternoon tea in the Pump Room.
The present Pump Room was built in 1796 when it was decided that a larger one was needed. Although Prince Hoare's statue of Beau Nash presides from one end of the hall, Nash himself died 32 years before this room was built. The chandelier is Victorian and has been described as "a set of instruments for an American band". It was taken down after the second war and replaced by one from the Assembly Rooms. The present chandelier was put up in 1959. No longer do waitresses serve out the waters from behind a bar at the pump. The stained glass has also been removed and the Victorian arches replaced by large windows more in keeping with the style of the rest of the room.

9 Although most of the cards in this book were printed after 1902 (when the Post Office finally allowed both address and message to be written on the reverse) many earlier photographs were used as postcards. This one, for example, shows the Roman Baths, shortly after their discovery in 1887. It had been known that Roman ruins existed in Bath, but they were not discovered until the 1880's when leaks to the King's Bath were being investigated. The colonnade and terrace now surrounding the Roman Baths were built in 1897 to J M Brydon's design. The billiard room in the background has now been demolished, leaving an open space on the south side of the abbey.

10/11 A statue of King Bladud, the legendary founder of Bath, can be seen at the top right corner of this picture of the King's Bath; the inscription below it, of 1699, describes him as "a great philosopher and Mathematician. Bred at Athens and recorded the first discoverer and founder of these baths, eight hundred and sixty three years before Christ." Built about 1100 AD the King's Bath was named after Henry I, the sovereign at that time. Most of the surrounding stonework as seen

here is Victorian but it has recently been restored and tidied up. The hot spring, which rises directly under this bath, is 49°C.

12 A summer afternoon about 1904 in Stall Street, outside the King & Queen's baths.
The colonnade and entrance to the baths were built in 1786, designed by Thomas Baldwin. The head in the oval wreath, flanked by sphinxes, on the pediment, is Hygeia, the Goddess of Health. The ornate pavilion at the end, and the upper storey, were added in 1886 by C. E. Davis, an architect whose modernisations and "improvements" of the 1880's have been heavily criticized as being completely tasteless, perhaps not without justification. The south wing has recently been rebuilt in the original style, and is now the official souvenir and gift shop.

13 This elaborate pavilion, housing the public mineral water fountain, was designed by Stephano Pieroni in 1859. There was originally a statue in the middle, supposedly of Bladud. The fountain has changed considerably and the railings have been removed.

14 The Royal Baths, in the southern wing of the Grand Pump Room Hotel (an attractive extra to this already luxurious hotel) were connected by a network of tunnels to the Pump Room and treatment centre so that residents and those here for a 'cure' could be conveyed in the utmost comfort and luxury to all essential ports of call. This photograph was probably taken in the late 1920's. Note the florist's barrow next to the fountain.

15 The Grand Pump Room Hotel as seen from the Abbey Churchyard, possibly around the end of the nineteenth century. As can be seen it was rather overpowering for its situation, directly facing the Abbey. Nevertheless it was described in "Ports of the Bristol Channel" in 1893 as "a remarkably handsome and commodious edifice." It was built in the French Rennaissance style in 1869 on the site of the White Hart Hotel, made famous by Dickens in "The Pickwick Papers". For 70 years it provided "all that is luxurious and elegant in modern hotel appointment" until it was requisitioned for government offices in the Second World War. In 1947 British Railways bought it but it was not re-established as a hotel and was eventually pulled down in 1959 and replaced by a block of shops and offices in a slightly more modest style. This card was printed in Germany, which was the centre of the early picture postcard industry, producing high quality, well-printed and coloured cards.

16 An ambitious card by a local printer, posted in 1906, the card below is unusual in being printed in French, catering for the foreign tourist.

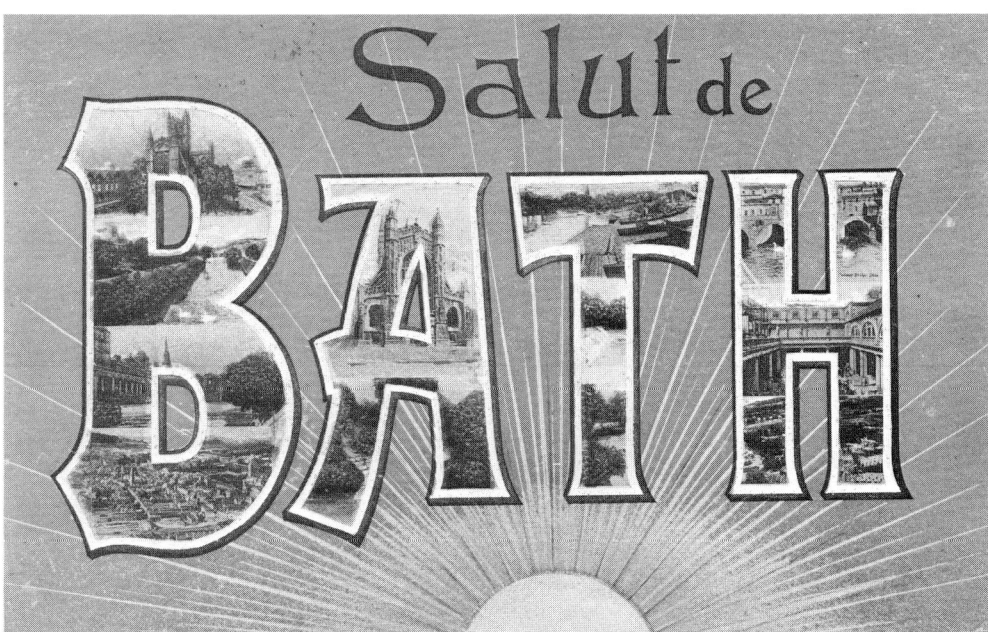

17 Designed by John Wood, the Mineral Water Hospital was commenced in 1738. At a time when people were flocking to Bath to be cured, this hospital was built to accommodate them. A piece of ground was acquired in Upper Borough Walls, on the site of the Old Playhouse (closed as a result of an Act of Parliament suppressing theatres). The new west block, seen towards the right of this picture, was built in 1859. By this time over 39,000 patients had attended the hospital, a large proportion of whom had had considerable relief or been completely cured. Queen Victoria gave permission for the name to be changed to the Royal Mineral Water Hospital in 1887. It is now known as the Royal National Hospital for Rheumatic Diseases.

18 The medieval St James' Church was rebuilt in the 1760's to a design by John Palmer in the Georgian Gothic style. G. R. Manners rebuilt most of it in 1848, giving it a more Classical appearance. The church was completely gutted in the German raids of 1942 and was demolished. The site is occupied today by Woolworths. The vicar, the Rev. F. Garfield Waterbury, shown here, came to office in 1930.

19/20 H. & R. Marsh's shop on the left of this card is still in existence but Beasley and Crocker's cash drapers is now the offices of the South Western Electricity Board. This and the view below were probably taken about the same time, ie. 1905. The Southgate Street scene can be dated by the scaffolding in place around the Abbey pinnacles which were replaced between 1904 and 1906. St James' Church, in the centre is not the only building to have disappeared from this view. The site is now occupied by an ultra-modern shopping precinct, built in the 1960's, the object of much controversy, as it came at a time when people were only just becoming aware of Bath's valuable heritage, and making more of an effort to preserve it.

21 Norfolk Crescent is part of a group of buildings named to commemorate Nelson's victory in 1798 (Norfolk was his home county). Others were Nelson Place and Nile Street, nearby. At one time this was a graceful, fashionable area with a charming view over the river. All that changed with the coming of the railway with its attendant noise and dirt, and then the building of the gas works on the other side of the river.

22 The Midland Railway Station was opened on 7th May 1870. Its name was changed several times, from Queen Square to Midland Station, LMS Station and finally Green Park Midland Station. The front is a fine example of Victorian classical architecture. It is now disused but being a listed building it is hoped that it will be preserved and re-used. Numerous schemes have been put forward including a hypermarket, an hotel and a tropical hothouse.

23   This view was probably taken between 1918 and 1920 as on close examination two soldiers can be seen walking up Westgate Street. Most of the buildings in Kingsmead Square were designed by Strahan in the 1730's, and restoration was started in 1974.

24   The building of the New Theatre Royal was started in 1802, designed by George Dance. It opened in October 1805 with 'Richard III'. The entrance was then in Beaufort Square. In 1862 the theatre was gutted by fire and was rebuilt, incorporating four houses behind (St John's Court, one of which had been occupied by Beau Nash) and the entrance was moved to Sawclose. The building on the left was a public house specialising in cockles and other sea food, named the "Peep O'Day" after the last play to be performed in the old theatre. The new entrances to the stalls, next to the Garrick's Head, on the left hand side of the theatre, were probably built in the '20's or '30's.

25 John Wood's famous Queen Square, named after Queen Caroline, George II's consort, was begun in 1729 and finished 7 years later. Many famous people have lived here including Dr Oliver of "Bath Oliver" biscuit fame, and John Wood himself, but in the 1900's, as nowadays, the square was mostly occupied by hotels and solicitors. However, much else has changed in Queen Square and it is no longer quite the green haven in the city centre that it seems in this picture. Cars roar about it as around a motorway roundabout and the railings have long since disappeared, the grass trampled away by people taking diagonal short cuts across the square.

26 This building has apparently been given over to alcoholic pursuits for most of its life. In the nineteenth century it was "The Raven" public house. Fullers 'established 1880', according to the emblem on the wall outside, remained open, as wine merchants or a public house until just before the second World War and the building is now a pub called Hatchetts. This photograph was probably taken around 1906, judging by the style of suit worn by the gentleman on the left.

27   Milsom Street, built in the 1760's, was originally a residential street with houses of a uniform and graceful frontage. It was not long until it began to become a shopping thoroughfare. By the early years of this century, as seen in this picture, it had become a fashionable and busy shopping centre and has remained so ever since. On the left can be seen horse cabs waiting for shoppers. These cabs survived in Bath until the 1930's. On the right in the foreground is a boy selling posies of flowers from a basket.

28   Edgar buildings, on the left of the view below, were part of the original plan including Milsom Street. The canopy over the pavement is the entry to the Constitutional Club and further down are Bartholemews Turkish Baths. The York House Hotel on the right housed various members of royalty, including Queen Victoria, throughout the nineteenth century. Next to the hotel is the Post Office, now sited at the corner of New Bond Street and Broad Street.

29/30 All the streets of Bath were extravagantly decorated for the Pageant of 1909. This display in George Street would have been designed to be seen along the whole of Milsom Street and must have looked very impressive. In both these cards typically Edwardian policemen can be seen posing for the camera. Among the shops to be seen in Union Street are S. Fox-Andrews, Grocer and Wine Merchants and Colmers', "the great ready money drapers".

This was the heyday of the picture postcard and cards were photographed and printed almost within a matter of hours, providing a document of all major social and political events. The card of Union Street was posted on the 22nd of July, just 4 days after it was photographed. Its sender tells of what a "grand sight it is to be here this week". The postal system, being much more efficient than it is nowadays, made it possible for cards to be the equivalent of our 'phone calls (but costing only a $\frac{1}{2}$d a time) and one could send a card in the morning to invite a friend to tea the same day.

31/32 On 31st March 1911 a public meeting was held in the Guildhall to decide on the way the City should celebrate the coronation of George V in June of that year, and these decorations outside the Pump Room are evidently the result of that meeting. The card is a re-touched day scene, a popular way of providing variety on post cards at that time.

Below is the proclamation of George V outside the Guildhall on 10th May 1910. This photograph was taken maybe one hour or so before the event took place and the crowd had not yet grown to its full size. The children, in their Sunday best had been given places at the front of the crowd so that they would not miss anything. The two men in the foreground on the right look as though they might be pickpockets, discussing their next victim!

33 On the left is the Mayor's Swordbearer, who was present at official functions. There have been five swordbearers this century, t[he] present one being Mr Eady, and this is the first one, Mr Hale, appoint[ed] 1st April 1900.

34 The Corridor was built in 1825, and designed by Goodridge a[nd] the glass roof was put in in 1870. William Friese-Greene, a pioneer [of] photography had his studio at No. 7. the Corridor in the late nineteen[th] century. By the time of this picture he had moved, and anoth[er] photographer had taken over the studio. At No. 5, on the left, is Miss Ford Haywood's ladies hairdresser and perfumer.

35 The Suffragette Movement had quite a following in Bath, possibly because these two leading figures in the Women's Social and Political Union, Lady Constance Lytton, (grand-daughter of Bulwer Lytton, 18th Century novelist and Bath resident), and Mrs Pethick-Lawrence, had connections with the area. Lady Constance became involved with the Women's Movement in 1905 and met Mrs Pethick Lawrence and also Annie Kenney (a mill hand from the North of England, who although working class had quite a gift for oratory). Each time Lady Constance and other women were arrested for causing a disturbance she realised that she was being unfairly given preferential treatment because of her rank, so she disguised herself and was committed to Walton Jail in October 1909 under the name Jane Warton. After going on hunger strike she was force-fed and very badly treated before being released. She later wrote a book about her experiences which did a lot to bring the women's plight to the public eye. This poster is probably for a meeting in 1910. The photographer, it seems, had a sly sense of humour and managed to include the words "Lord what fools these mortals be" from another poster below.

36 Flags were flying at the Guildhall during Pageant week in 1909. The tram in the foreground served as an information office for visitors to the Pageant. The main part of the Guildhall dates from 1776 and was designed by Baldwin. The Art gallery and library extension, round the corner in Bridge Street, was added in the 1890's by Brydon.

37   Ordinary double decker trams were too high to go through the arch by the Green Tree on the Oldfield Park Route, and so special single decker trams, like this one, had to be used. This photograph was taken in the latter days of the tram's life in Bath, in the 1930's.

38   Nowadays, owing to recent restoration and cleaning, and the removal of such things as the placard advertising Madame Hamilton (corset and belt maker) on the central pavilion, Pulteney Bridge looks far more elegant and impressive than as shown in this postcard of 1909. Designed by Robert Adam it was built 1769 to '74 and was his only work in Bath. From the same spot today one would have a view of the new weir of 1972 curving up towards the bridge.

39 Work was started on Laura Place and Pultney Street, part of William Johnstone Pulteney's proposed Bathwick estate, in the 1780's. The fountain in the centre was added in 1877 but removed after World War II. Its remains are now being used as a flower bed. This photograph from the 1930's shows the replacement of the horse drawn cabs by motor taxis.

The trees lining Pulteney Street were recently removed, the excuse being that they were old and that the roots were causing damage.

40 This picture of the interior of the Pultney Hotel, the entrance of which is visible on the left above, gives a good impression of Edwardian Bath, described by Bryan Little as a scene of, "opulent visitors ensconced and cossetted amid the potted palms of large luxurious hotels. It was still the time for lap dogs and ladies' maids". The hotel was established in the 1860's and the "notable prosperity of the establishment" was due, according to an account of 1893, to the proprietors', "assiduous care for the comfort of their guests, many of whom belong to the most distinguished families, and to the excellent situation and luxurious appointments of the house". So it continued until 1946 when the hotel was requisitioned by the Ministry of National Insurance for use as offices.

41 A meeting was held on May 15th 1915, "to consider the desirability of establishing a club in connection with the Bowling Green just completed in Sydney Gardens." This picture of a very successful-looking team was probably taken in the 1920's.

42 This view of the boating station in Forester Road presents a picture of an archetypally idyllic Edwardian summer afternoon on the river (shades of "Three Men in a Boat"!) Unfortunately the view from the river is no longer as green and rural as it then was.

43 The present post-office, opened in 1927 is situated on the corner to the left of this picture. St Michael's Church itself was Bath's Post Office in Ralph Allen's time, before he moved it from the disused church's nave to his house in Lilliput Alley. There has been a church here since the Middle Ages. It was rebuilt in the eighteenth century and again in 1836 in the 'Gothick' revival style by G. P. Manners.

44 An exotic display of tropical fruits and flowers is presented in the window of W. Vilven in New Bond Street. Well might some of nearby Milsom Street's prosperous clientele have been tempted by a pineapple or a coconut. Nowadays, there is nothing more exciting than a school outfitters' to catch one's eye when passing this spot.

45/46 The last tram in Bath ran on May 6th 1939 from the Guildhall to the depot in Walcot Street, shown here probably in the last decade before the trams disappeared. On its final journey the tram was driven by the Mayor and souvenir tickets (the fare was 1½d) were issued in leather wallets.

Bath Electric Tramways Ltd. had taken over from the Bath Omnibus and Road Car company, which operated the horse trams, when electric trams were first introduced in 1904.

Below is the tram terminus at Weston. The house in the background next to the church was where one Mr Gregory, a carpenter lived.

CAMDEN CRESCENT & HEDGEMEAD PARK.   BATH.

47 Owing to several rather alarming subsidences Camden Crescent, begun in 1788 was never completed. In 1875 there was an even larger landslip. All remaining houses in the area directly below the Cresent were demolished and Hedgemead Park was planted. In July 1889 the park was opened to the public. Standing on this spot today the view of Camden Crescent, and below it Ainslie's Belvedere and Caroline Place, is completely obscured by full-grown trees.

48 Electric street lights, trams and a motor garage had arrived in the same area only a few years after the picture above was taken. The garage belonged to Mr F. C. Wallace. The horse and cart may possibly be delivering petrol or oil. St Swithin's church, on the left, was the work of John Palmer and was opened in 1780.

HEDGEMEAD PARK, BATH.

49 This view of Cleveland Bridge was taken about ten years before it was freed from the toll in 1927. The buildings in this area seem to be mostly devoted to chemistry; on the corner is Sampson's, a chemists' to this day. Further towards the bridge is the Bath & West of England College of Chemistry and Pharmacy, next door Percy Thompson, analytical chemist and finally the Eastern dispensary.

50 The block of buildings on the right was rebuilt in 1900, presumably as part of the general reorganization of the area after the Hedgemead landslip. This view of Walcot was taken from outside Hedgemead Park in about 1905. The public house, the Hat and Feather, on the far right is still very much in existence, as is the hardware shop next door, under a new proprietor.

51 Grosvenor Place, designed by John Eveleigh, is described by Ison in "Georgian Buildings of Bath" as "one of the most exciting buildings in Bath". The central building was originally intended to be a hotel. By the time of this photograph it was the Grosvenor College for Ladies and now it suffers the fate of being a furniture repository. In the same block were Claremont Girls' School and the Victoria College for Girls. Grosvenor Place is separated from the London Road by a band of trees several yards wide and its own carriage road.

52 This view of Lambridge (almost directly opposite Grosvenor Place) with a tram heading out for Bathford is beautifully evocative of the atmosphere of a misty, wintry day.

53 Brock St forms an extremely unostentatious link between the Circus and Royal Crescent and so enables one to get a fuller sense of their grandeur. Halfway down on the left can be seen Shirley and Ridge, grocers and wine merchants, on the corner of Margaret's Buildings.

54 The view of Belvedere today, from the same spot is virtually the same as this one of circa 1918. The post office on the right is still there, as is Cornish, the butcher, opposite. Miss Smith's, confectioner, next door down the hill, is now one of many antique shops in the area, but the chemists' shop, with a lantern outside and the greengrocer's next door are still there, albeit under different management.

Landsdown Crescent, Bath.

/56 Arguably the pleasantest crescent in Bath, if not as grand as
[Ro]yal Crescent, is Lansdown Cresent, erected between 1789 and 1793 to
[Pa]lmer's designs. The house at the end, with an arch joining it to the
[ne]xt house, was occupied during the early nineteenth century by
[W]illiam Beckford, the eccentric millionaire and author of the 'Gothick'
[no]vel "Vathek". He moved to Bath after selling his impressive home,
[Fo]nthill Abbey in Wiltshire and proceeded to landscape magnificently
[th]e stretch of land he owned behind the Crescent, culminating in a
[to]wer on the top of Lansdown Hill, a mile or so away. The upper storey
[of] this tower is seen below, in about 1920, complete with sightseers who,
[th]en as now, could climb the 156 steps and survey an impressive view of
[Ba]th and its surroundings.

Beckford Tower, Lansdown Bath.

57/58 The Assembly Rooms, designed by John Wood the younger, were an immensely popular venue for balls and soirées when they opened in 1771, but by the end of the nineteenth century they had begun to lose a lot of money. During the First World War they were used for aviation work and from 1921 the premises were a cinema. By 1930 they were in a very bad state, but luckily the Society for the Protection of Ancient Buildings were able to buy the Rooms with an anonymous donation. They were restored under the direction of the National Trust with Mowbray Green as architect and were re-opened on October 18th 1938 with a Grand gala ball, in aid of the Mineral Water Hospital and attended by H.R.H. the Duchess of Kent. These photographs were taken shortly before the re-opening. Unfortunately the Assembly Rooms were completely gutted by fire only four years later in the "Baedeker" raids that damaged so many other beautiful buildings in Bath. However the Rooms have once more been restored to their former glory.

59 Rivers Street, (so called because Sir Henry Rivers once resided there, at number 18) was part of the general extension of building behind the Assembly Rooms carried out by John Wood the Younger between about 1770 and 1780. At Number 3, (foreground left in this postcard) lived William Savage Landor, the poet and writer. At the time of this picture it was occupied by the Misses Lane. There appears to be a 'gentleman caller' about to knock on their door. In the middle of the street two road sweepers lean on their brooms to stare at the camera, still a great novelty in 1915.

60 Francis' Hotel had another branch in Queen Square, as seen in number 66. Established in 1883, it changed hands and became the Regina Hotel in 1933. Standing outside is the hotel's private horse bus or 'brake' which would meet patrons at the station. Several other hotels also had 'brakes' and the practice continued until the 1920's. Postcards at this time usually cost 1d, but cards such as this one, advertising a hotel or a theatre performance, for instance, cost less.

The Circus. Bath Built by the elder Wood in 1754, and reckons among the finest architecture in Bath. Many eminent men have had their residence here, among whom was William Pitt Earl of Chatham.

61/62 The Circus, one of John Wood's great architectural works, was begun in 1754. John Wood died a few months after work was begun, and it was completed by his son. Based on a Roman Amphitheatre it was originally known as the King's Circus. As can be seen from the photograph below, many of the acorn ornaments topping the parapet were missing until a few years ago. The railing around the central green disappeared, along with most other iron railings in Bath, to make guns in the war. It can be seen from old prints of the Circus that it was originally completely paved over, without the massive plane trees which have been deplored by so many architectural historians as destroying the whole effect of the Circus. At the time this picture was taken most of the residents of the Circus were doctors or surgeons. Perhaps the two Bath chairs are waiting for patients consulting their physicians?

BATH. The Circus.

/64 After finishing the Circus, the younger John Wood moved on to
Royal Crescent, possibly the most famous of Bath's great pieces of
architecture. In the 1900's some of Bath's most distinguished residents
lived here; almost every entry in the local directory is an O.B.E., Lady,
Countess or Right Honorable.

A strange intrusion to those familiar with the view of the Crescent
nowadays is the spire of St. Andrew's church, shown below, which was
destroyed in the air raids of 1942. This church was built in the 1870's,
designed by Sir George Gilbert Scott—the only Victorian architect to
have designed a whole church in Bath. The style was somewhat out of
keeping with the rest of Bath's Victorian building, which tended to conform more to the classical models already set down.

65 Time has so faded this photograph of a procession in 1911 that it is impossible to ascertain from the banner whether this was the Salvation Army, a Temperance Society, a military band or a trade union meeting. At any rate, there seems to be a large crowd of people in their Sunday best enjoying the spectacle.

66 A party pose for the camera before setting off on their charabanc outing. Large as the vehicle is, it is hard to imagine them all fitting in. In the background is Queen Square and Francis Hotel. This picture was probably taken around 1920.

BATH MILITARY BAND.
Mr. W. F. C. Schottler, Conductor.

67/68 Founded in May 1817, the Bath Military Band gave summer concerts for 100 years until 1917 when an orchestra took over. They gave three evening concerts a week in the summer from the bandstand in Victoria Park; Wednesday, Friday and a free one on Mondays. They are seen here, in 1906, seated in the bandstand with their conductor, Mr W. F. C. Schottler. Below is the avenue in the park, during a performance lined with concertgoers awaiting cabs.

69 Historical pageants were a very fashionable part of Edwardian life, and many breathtaking spectacles with gorgeous costumes and casts of thousands were seen all over the country. In these pre-television days it was considered that historians of the future would look back in reverence to the age that produced such an excellent way of not only entertaining but educating as well. The Bath Pageant of 1909 was produced entirely by local effort; all the costumes and sets were made by volunteers, the 2,500 strong cast were all Bathonians and the words and music were by local composers.

Thousands of people from all over Britain flocked to Bath for the Pageant week, and the tramcar above served as an information office to deal with their enquiries.

70 Miss Powell of Bath, Ontario and Miss Taylor of Bath, New Brunswick were the Canadian, "Daughters of Bath" who posed in a tableau centering around "Mother Bath" and including twelve other girls from American towns named Bath.

71 The history of Bath was told in eight episodes, beginning with the Roman occupation, moving on to the crowning of King Edgar, Elizabeth I's visit and the days of Beau Nash. The legend of Bladud's discovery of the hot springs, with the help of his pigs, was included in the Elizabethan episode.

72 Despite the elaborate costumes, this "group of Elizabethan ladies" looks very solidly Edwardian.

73 The Pageant was managed and produced by Mr Frank Lascelles, an internationally famous stage manager. At the end of the Pageant a presentation was made to him by the Duke and Duchess of Connaught, the Pageant's Royal patrons.

74 The culmination of the Pageant was a grand procession along Milsom St. The crowds of "loyal citizens" seen below must have been overwhelming; Bath has probably never seen anything like it before or since.

75 It was at this house, in the eighteenth century, that Sally Lunn made her famous teacakes. Lilliput Alley is now less romantically named North Parade Passage. Dated 1482, Sally Lunn's house is often claimed to be the oldest house in Bath, but in fact the Abbey Church House is probably older. At the beginning of this century the house was variously a bakers', a grocers', a private home and a tea-shop. Then in 1938, when this photograph was taken, Mary Byng-Johnson, an artist, took up residence and had her studio there. She died in 1965 after, it is said, having seen a ghost. The present tea-shop opened soon after.

76 Opened in November 1901, the Empire Hotel has been described by local historian Brian Little as "a fearful mock-Jacobean skyscraper with a touch of Lacock Abbey in the top corner." At the time it was probably regarded as the last word in modern luxurious hotels. This picture, taken a few years after its opening shows the rank of horse cabs waiting for hotel guests. The obelisk in Orange Grove was erected in 1734 by Beau Nash to commemorate a visit by the Prince of Orange.

77 The building of North Parade Bridge in 1835 ended North Parade's status as a cul-de-sac. It was started by Tierney Clark, who was the engineer of London's Hammersmith Bridge. On this bright summer day three Edwardian schoolgirls lean over the parapet, admiring the view of the river.

78 On the right of the view below is the old police station in Orange Grove. Opened in 1866, it was in operation for just over a hundred years before the new police station in Manvers Street was opened. Over in the High Street, the shops with white blinds are W. Cornish the butcher and on the corner, William H. Smith, trunk and portmanteau makers.

76   BATH. — The Orange Grove and Police Station. — LL.

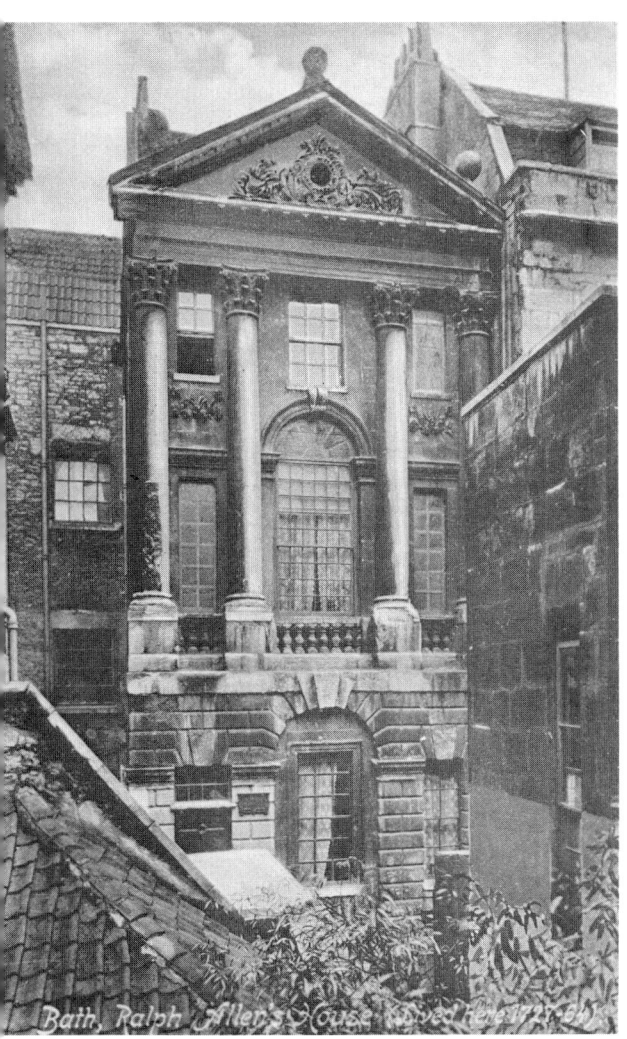

79/80 Ralph Allen not only played a large part in shaping eighteenth century Bath, but also reformed the mail a great deal, improving the system of cross posts (which allowed local letters to go direct from town to town instead of via London). Without his work one could almost say that postcards, as they were in the 1900s—a speedy, convenient form of communication—could never have come about. Allen started his career in the Post Office at the age of eleven in his native Cornwall. He came to Bath in 1719 and amassed a moderate amount of money from his management of the cross posts. His house in Lilliput Alley, shown here, was partly designed by John Wood. It was to this house in 1725 that he transferred the Post Office from the old St. Michael's Church.

He bought Hampton Manor in 1730 and began to exploit the beds of stone there. Bath stone was not popular outside Bath at this time, and it is said that his grand country house, Prior Park, was built to illustrate the hard wearing properties of Bath stone. Whether that was so or not, Allen made his fortune from his stone quarries. He became legendary for his kindness and generosity, giving large sums to charity and the Bath Hospitals.

The reverse of the card below, of 1906, reads, "Our Mr Jelly hopes to have the pleasure of calling upon you on Monday next when the favour of your esteemed orders will greatly oblige. Your obedient servants, The Bath Stone Firms Ltd."

81/82 In the distance, to the left of this view, a glimpse can be caught between two church spires of Prior Park, Ralph Allen's magnificent country house. In the centre is North Parade, where another postal pioneer, John Palmer, lived in the eighteenth century. His contribution to speeding the post was to suggest that, as the roads had been greatly improved, mail could be carried on coaches instead of by a post boy or horse. The first mail coach ran in 1784. From this time the post became very fast and reliable.

In the foreground can be seen the roof of the Royal Literary and Scientific Institute, the facade of which can be seen below. Opened in 1825, the Institute was quite a cultural centre and focus for the arts in the West Country. In the 1930s it was decided to demolish this building to make way for a traffic "improvement". The collection was moved to Queen Square in 1932, to the building now occupied by the Reference Library. During the war the Admiralty took over the premises and the books and specimens were put into storage. The Institute never regained its former glory after the war, not least of the reasons being lack of premises. The picture below right can be dated at about 1905 from the scaffolding still in position on the Abbey tower, replacing the damaged pinnacles.

83 Guinea Pig Jack, in his scarlet coat, was a familiar sight in Manvers Street for many years until he died in 1907 aged 75. This photograph was taken a year or two before his death. His real name was Dominice Oconia and he came to Bath from Italy in 1848. After selling newspapers for a short time he found it more lucrative to stage street corner shows of performing guinea pigs.

84 Brunel's Great Western Railway opened between Bath and Bristol in 1840, the link with London not being completed until 1841. The coming of the railway led to quite a revolution in Bath's industrial importance and brought plenty of new trade. Bath expanded rapidly, and by 1901 the population was double that of a century before. By the time of this photograph, 1919–20, it would have been even more.

85/86. There has been a bridge leading into Bath from the Wells road since 1362, when it was known as St Lawrence's Bridge. This was rebuilt in the eighteenth century and in the nineteenth century the road was widened and the footpaths cantilevered on each side, as can be seen in the above picture. The Old Bridge has now been replaced by the modern Churchill Bridge: the Full Moon and other riverfront buildings have all disappeared to make way for the Electricity Board's offices and car parks. In many ways the view below is reminiscent of Amsterdam today, with its bridges, trams and ornate church spires.

87   This card, of the Seven Stars in Avon Buildings, Twerton (a mile or so from the city centre) presents a mystery. The message on the back reads, "Dear John, I hope you will like this card as it's part of the Old Home.", but researches have failed to discover which "home" it refers to. Perhaps it was once the sender's family home or an orphanage. The other buildings are a brewery, a maltsters and D. Harris' greengrocer's shop.

88   The old Bear Inn, on the Wells road (shown here in 1914) at one time had its own brewery. The bear on the sign was painted by a Mr Cross who apparently painted best when drunk, according to local legend!

89   The Kennet and Avon canal, joining Bristol and Reading, was the most ambitious of the eighteenth century navigations, owing to the great fall and thus the number of locks from the canal to the river. Opened in 1810, its traffic was never as heavy as had been anticipated, and by the end of the century it had declined greatly, a process speeded by the direct competition of the railway. The railway company eventually bought the canal but standards of maintenance were not kept up and by 1918, (about the time of this picture) some parts could only be navigated with difficulty. After the last war it was completely closed but the recently formed Kennet and Avon Canal Trust has succeeded, with the help of volunteer labour, in restoring much of the canal, including the Widcombe lock flight, shown here, which was recently re-opened.

90   There has been great controversy over who designed Widcombe Manor but it is generally supposed to have been Inigo Jones. Built for the Lord of the Manor in the early eighteenth century, it passed to the Bennett family, and by the time this picture was taken (about 1905) it was occupied by a Mrs Pyle and a Mrs Garde-Brown.

© Felicity Bowers
& Karl Jaeger

Kingsmead Press

Reproduced and printed by photolithography and bound in Great Britain at The Bath Press, Avon